THE SHE DEVOTIONAL:

31 Daily Inspirations for A Woman's Spirit, Health and Emotions

DR. SHANI K. COLLINS

Upper Level Publishing

The SHE Devotional: 31 Daily Inspirations for a Woman's Spirit, Health and Emotions™

Copyright © 2015 by Dr. Shani K. Collins

Upper Level Publishing, LLC., MS, USA

The cover image is used under license from Depositphotos.com

Scripture quotations are taken from the *Holy Bible*, New King James Version®. Copyright © 1982 by Thomas Nelson. Used by permission. All rights reserved.

This book is not intended as a substitute for the medical advice of physicians. The reader should regularly consult a physician in matters relating to his/her health and particularly with respect to any symptoms that may require diagnosis or medical attention.

ISBN: 978-0-9969233-0-9

If you would like the author to contact you about a speaking engagement, ask any questions about a speaking engagement, or obtain a quotation, please visit: www.shanicollins.com

10 9 8 7 6 5 4 3 2 1

CONTENTS

Acknowledgements

- I acknowledge Jesus Christ as my Lord and Savior. I thank God for speaking to my spirit years ago, and leading me to write my deepest thoughts. At the time, I did not know the devotionals would be used to develop *The SHE Devotional: 31 Daily Inspirations for a Woman's Spirit, Health and Emotions™*. I am grateful to God for the opportunity to spread His message of love, hope and forgiveness with others.

- To my parents, Charles and Cassie, and sister, Kanika, thank you for your unwavering commitment to any and everything I decide to undertake. You three are my "Dream Team," my biggest supporters, and my collective anchor during times of trouble. I love you all to the moon and back. Mom, thank you for always telling me to write a book.

- To my brother-in-law, Reggie, thank you for your constant love and support.

- To my favorite little babies, Sidney and Reginald, thank you for inspiring your aunt on a daily basis. I love you.

- To my dear brothers, Charles and Michael, and Jamie you hold a special place in my heart. I love you.

- To my many aunts, uncles, cousins, and extended family members from the Osborne family and the Collins family, thank you for your love and ongoing support.

- To the pastors and members of the following churches: Friendship Missionary Baptist Church in Greenwood, Mississippi; Antioch Baptist Church in Atlanta, Georgia; and Elizabeth Missionary Baptist Church in Tuscaloosa, Alabama, thank you for praying for me. Your steadfast prayers, encouragement, and support have meant the world to me. Without the spiritual teaching and encouragement I have received from you throughout the years, this book would not be possible.

- To Lisa, thank you dearly for the work you put into editing my book and working with my busy schedule.

- To Angie, thank you for the amazing book cover design.

- To my many personal, professional, and academic friends and mentors, thank you for your ongoing support.

- To Marcia, thank you for being a steadfast friend. You are a true blessing.

- To my love, Timothy, my *Good Soldier*, you have shown me what it means to walk with a Godly, supportive, loving, and encouraging man of principle. Thank you for reassuring me during this process and for supporting me.

- To my many Facebook, Instagram and Twitter friends, I appreciate the constant support and online engagement. Thank you.

- To the many individuals who purchased *The SHE Devotional: 31 Daily Inspirations for a Woman's Spirit, Health and Emotions™*, thank you very much. May the daily inspirations in this book help you increase and mature in your walk with Christ.

INTRODUCTION

I would describe myself as a busy woman. In fact, busy women such as mothers, daughters, wives, faith and worship leaders, church goers, entrepreneurs, businesswomen, caregivers, and students inspired me to write *The SHE Devotional: 31 Daily Inspirations for a Woman's Spirit, Health and Emotions™*. Busy women often struggle to balance work, family, and personal responsibilities. Busy women can also neglect their relationship with God, neglect their personal health (e.g., fail to maintain a healthy diet and engage in regular exercise), and neglect to manage their emotions in a healthy way. During my years as a graduate student, I was guilty of neglecting three areas of self-care: my spirit, my health, and my emotions.

I encourage you to use *The SHE Devotional™* as a tool to help you address three key areas of self-care: your Spirit (S), your Health (H), and your Emotions (E). I think when one of these areas is out of sync in a woman's life, it impacts the other two areas of her life. *The SHE Devotional™* gives you a three-in-one experience. It consists of 31 daily devotionals to help you connect with God, 31 tips to help you improve your physical health, and 31 practical steps to help you better manage your emotions. As a bonus, this book also includes 31 inspirational songs to motivate and encourage you each day, a 40-day prayer journal for you to write your thoughts, and a helpful index of scriptures and inspirational songs for your convenience. Some of the daily inspirations you will read in this book were written at critical points in my life. I am happy to share with you what I learned about God's faithfulness during the peaks and the valleys of my own life. Other devotionals are simply messages that God impressed upon my spirit.

While enrolled in a doctoral program, I would read devotionals and inspirational books by Christian authors like Dr. Charles Stanley, Joyce Meyer, Bishop T.D. Jakes, Beth Moore, Max Lucado, Stormie Omartian, and Joel Osteen. Why? Sometimes, my extremely busy schedule prevented me from having in depth bible study sessions. Yet, I still desired to connect with God on a daily basis. I recall reading devotionals while walking to class, in preparation for a test, in preparation for a job interview, and in preparation for intense meetings. I love devotionals. I still read them and carry them with me each day. However, I do not use them as a substitute for reading God's Holy Word, instead they provide me with small pieces God's wisdom. I encourage you to read the Word of God for yourself. Use this book as a supplement.

It is my prayer that *The SHE Devotional*™ inspires you to find time to connect with God and cultivate your personal relationship with Him, take measurable steps to improve your health, and live a life that is led by the Holy Spirit, not by your emotions. Please, read this book as many times as you would like. Carry it with you each day. Share it with a friend. Most of all, enjoy the process of connecting with God each day, improving your personal health, and discovering new ways to experience more emotional and spiritual peace in your life.

With Love,

Shani

Day One

WHEN YOU ARE TIRED

*And he said unto me, My grace is sufficient for thee:
for my strength is made perfect in weakness.
Most gladly therefore will I rather glory in my infirmities,
that the power of Christ may rest upon me.*

2 Corinthians 12:9

Spirit: Life can drain you. The daily demands of family, work, school, travel, and social obligations can leave you feeling tired, angry, frustrated, and even depressed. It may appear as though the *rat race* of life will never end. Be encouraged: God's word confirms that when you are weak, He is strong. Because God promises to be your strength, you don't have to take on the task of *saving the world,* a task that many women often try to undertake. As a woman of God, recognize that being overworked is not God's purpose for your life. Why? When you are tired and overworked, it is hard to hear God's voice. You may not be able to change your daily work and family responsibilities, but you can change your outlook on those things.

You can change your outlook on challenging responsibilities by committing yourself only to the things God desires you to do. You will know His will when you pray for direction and guidance in your life. When you hear God's voice, He will

1

tell you what things to continue and what things to release. He promises in His word that if you will trust in Him with all your heart, He will direct your path (Proverbs 3:5). Therefore, surrender your tiredness, your frustrations, your stress, and the feeling of being overwhelmed, to God. He knows how you feel. He is your Heavenly Father and will be there to comfort you whenever you need to be renewed.

Health: Make a plan to go to bed early. Don't work on any extra projects. Give your body the rest it needs. If you must work, sit in complete silence for 30 minutes before proceeding. Turn off your phone. Don't respond to emails. Don't update social media sites. Simply sit in complete silence and slowly inhale and exhale. This will help you relax. It will reenergize you and give your body an extra boost.

Emotions: Being tired can have a negative impact on your emotions. You may find yourself lashing out at others and/or deeply frustrated. Instead of lashing out at others, take time to do some soul searching. Get in touch with your feelings and get your emotions in order. You can do this by journaling. Write down what you are feeling (e.g., *I am frustrated because I have been working overtime for three weeks*). Once you identify the source of your anger and/or frustration, you can work toward better managing your stressors. Once you identify and manage your stressors, you will feel a greater sense of control over your life. Subsequently, you will feel less tired and frustrated.

Prayer: Dear Father, today I release my tiredness, my frustrations, and my stress to you. I place my life in your capable hands. I repent of any anger, malice, and bitterness in my heart. Renew my spirit, my health, and my emotions, and lead me toward a peaceful daily walk with you. In Jesus' name, Amen.

Inspirational Song: "I Need You Now" by Smokie Norful

Day Two

EXPERIENCING JOY

Then he said unto them, Go your way, eat the fat, and drink the sweet, and send portions unto them for whom nothing is prepared: for this day is holy unto our LORD: neither be ye sorry; for the joy of the LORD is your strength.

Nehemiah 8:10

Spirit: *Did* you wake up today feeling loved, feeling the presence of the Lord? God is an awesome God. This is not just a popular phrase, but the absolute truth. God has promised in His Word that He will never leave you nor forsake you (Deuteronomy 31:6). Isn't it a wonderful feeling to know that when you are happy, God is right there with you? Even on days when all is wrong with the world, you can still find a reason to smile because God loves you. He is walking with you and guiding you through your personal trouble. Therefore, delight in the Lord and find a way to be happy today. Make today a joyful experience. God has given you 24 hours in each day; make the most of them. Don't spend your time being negative or being around negative people. God has called you to so much more. He has called you to experience His joy!

Health: Share a healthy lunch or dinner with friends or family you have not spoken to in a while.

Emotions: Call, text, or email a friend or relative to catch up. Conversation and interaction with others can bring true joy to the soul.

Prayer: Dear Father, regardless of today's circumstances, I will find a way to be happy and have an attitude of joy. In Jesus' name, Amen.

Inspirational Song: "I Smile" by Kirk Franklin

Day Three

FORGIVING OTHERS

For if ye forgive men their trespasses, your heavenly Father will also forgive you.
But if ye forgive not men their trespasses, neither will your Father forgive your trespasses.

Matthew 6:14-15

Spirit: Everyone makes mistakes. Yes, even you. Life's challenges are harder to deal with when you have an unforgiving heart and spirit. When you have the urge to fuss, gripe, and complain because things are not going your way, step away from the situation and take a moment of silence. Or, when you have the desire to give a person a piece of your mind, stop and reflect on the situation and think before you respond. God holds us accountable for our words and our actions. Most important, when you are upset, check your attitude. Each day, there will be countless opportunities for you to get mad, lose your cool, and respond to uncomfortable situations and unpleasant people in a hostile way. Instead of having a negative response, keep a forgiving sprit. By having a forgiving spirit, your response to such situations and people will be dramatically different.

God has called us to live in peace with one another. One of the best ways to honor God is to forgive those who have offended you, even if the offense is something that simply irritated or frustrated you. You may not change another person's behavior, but you can demonstrate actions that reflect your faith in God and your obedience to his principles on forgiveness.

Health: Living in anger and having an unforgiving spirit can cause your blood pressure to increase. Check your blood pressure today. You can do so at the local pharmacy or by scheduling a visit with your physician or nurse practitioner. High blood pressure can lead to serious health complications such as stroke, high cholesterol, and kidney damage. Reassess whether being unforgiving is really worth the cost.

Emotions: Having an unforgiving attitude is poison to the soul. If you are harboring bitterness toward someone who mistreated you, settle matters with that person in a Christian way. The first step toward reconciliation with others is prayer. Don't put off until tomorrow what you can do today.

Prayer: Dear Father, I am grateful that you have forgiven me. I repent for having an unforgiving heart and an attitude of resentment toward others. Give me a spirit to forgive others even when it is hard to do. In Jesus' name, Amen.

Inspirational Song: "Let Go" by DeWayne Woods

Day Four

DEDICATION

Brethren, I do not count myself to have apprehended; but one thing I do, forgetting those things which are behind and reaching forward to those things which are ahead, I press toward the goal for the prize of the upward call of God in Christ Jesus.

Philippians 3:13-14

Spirit: Working toward your goals takes a lot of mental, physical, emotional, and spiritual energy. It is God's power working in and through you that enables you to complete day-to-day tasks without faltering. Scripture teaches us: "Do not grow weary in doing well, for in due season you will reap the harvest if you faint not" (Galatians 6:9). Whatever God-given vision you have, pursue it with patience, with prayer, and with a heart dedicated to carrying out His will. God gives us ideas and blesses us with unique gifts and talents. He expects us to use our talents to bless the lives of others.

Whether your goal is to return to school, lose weight, finish a project, or hone your skills in a particular area, pursue the goal. God is right there with you every step of the way. Things will not always be easy. Committing to a larger purpose requires sacrifice, but if you will allow God to direct you, your journey will be prosperous in the end.

8

Health: Dedicate yourself to making a small, healthy change in your diet. Set a realistic goal for yourself such as reducing your fast food intake. Each day, make an effort to stick to your health goal. In no time, you will see your hard work paying off.

Emotions: Your dreams and goals begin with a thought and a vision. If you don't first believe in yourself, your vision will not come to pass. The Word of God encourages you to: "Write the vision, and make it plain upon tables, that he may run that readeth it" (Habakkuk 2:2). Create a vision board. It will help motivate you toward your goal. On your board, map out your path to success. Each week, work toward setting and completing goals that align with your personal vision.

Prayer: Dear Father, I thank you for blessing me with a diligent spirit to work toward my dreams and goals. When I feel lazy or burned out, send me your strength. Remind me to always keep your Word at the center of goals and dreams. Give me Godly confidence and when I am weak, reassure me that, I can do all things through your strength (Philippians 4:13). In Jesus' name, Amen.

Inspirational Song: "I Believe I Can Fly" by Yolanda Adams

Day Five

MANAGING YOUR PRIORITIES

*But seek ye first the kingdom of God, and his righteousness;
and all these things shall be added unto you.*

Matthew 6:33

Spirit: Do you frequently forget major events in your life? Do you miss playdates with your children? Do you miss family time at home? Do you miss church often? Are you neglectful in your prayer life? Are you frequently late for work? If so, you may need to readjust your priorities. Why? Living an unbalanced life can weaken your bonds with those closest to you (e.g., family, church family, co-workers).

God should be a priority in your life. God desires you to be a good steward of your time and the resources He has blessed you with. This involves knowing how to prioritize your time and your life responsibilities (e.g., faith, family, work, etc). As a woman of God, you are called to be a leader in your home, to be efficient in business, and to grow in Christ. Today, make time to shift your priorities so that all areas of your life work in sync, bring honor to God, and honor the personal and professional relationships you have established with others.

Health: Family is a top priority for many women. Make being healthy a fun, family effort. From the one mile kid's "fun run" to the actual 3.1 mile walk/run, 5K races are an exciting way for the whole family to bond and engage in a health related activity. Create a unique team name for your family and register for an upcoming 5K walk/run.

Emotions: Reflect on the ways that your busy schedule may have lead you to neglect your spiritual walk with Christ or your responsibilities at home or work. To get clarity on ways to slow down, you may simply need to physically stop, sit still, and reflect on your priorities. Silence can help you realign your priorities. Stillness is necessary to hear the voice of God. Open your mind and spirit to receiving God's instruction for your life. Listening to inspirational songs can help. Use the index of inspirational songs found at the back of this book to help you sit still and regroup.

Prayer: Dear Father, I thank you for helping me to recognize how busyness robs me of my peace of mind. Help me to hear your voice. Give me the wisdom to heed your warnings to slow down. Give me the wisdom to learn how to prioritize my life in such a way that I bring honor to you and to those around me. In Jesus' name, Amen.

Inspirational Song: "For Your Glory" by Tasha Cobbs

Day Six

MAKING POSITIVE CHANGES

If any man will come after me, let him deny himself,
And take up his cross daily, and follow me.

Luke 9:23

Spirit: What do you want to change in your life? Is it your job? Your weight? Your financial situation? Your love life? Your relationship with your parents? Whatever you desire to change about your life, you can do so through the power of God. Most women of God have areas in their lives that they desire to improve. However, for various reasons, you may find yourself wavering in your commitment to change. You may be holding onto behaviors and attitudes that God wishes to free you from.

God is willing to change you; however, you must be willing to be led by the Holy Spirit. God has given you His Word. It serves as a guide to help you recognize your shortcomings and your weaknesses. Thus, you are never alone in the process of becoming a better person. You may be struggling in a particular area because you have not surrendered the burden to God. God is very clear in His Word. He wants you to completely surrender your struggles and challenges to Him. Surrendering means laying down anything that would draw you away from Jesus Christ. When you are weak, God is strong (2 Corinthians 12:9). When you pray to Him, He will give you the spiritual insight to make the best decisions for your life.

Health: Focus on one bad habit you have resolved to break. Make a quick list of five reasons why you want to break that habit. Make a separate list of five challenges you have faced in breaking the habit. Make a list of five ways you can work toward finally breaking that bad habit.

Emotions: To make positive changes in your life, you must have a desire to change. A prideful attitude can destroy any progress toward change. Don't allow a prideful attitude to hold you back in life. Don't let it stop you from connecting with those who have the power to help you make positive changes.

Prayer: Dear Father, thank you for walking with me as I make changes in my life. Help me to grow spiritually and personally. Help me to surrender any unhealthy habits to you. In Jesus' name, Amen.

Inspirational Song: "He Wants It All" by Forever Young

Day Seven

YOUR CIRCLE OF INFLUENCE

*And do not be conformed to this world, but be transformed
by the renewing of your mind, that you may prove what is
that good and acceptable and perfect will of God.*

Romans 12:2

Spirit: *Your* success lies in your ability to recognize
negative influences in your life and separate from them. This
is a lesson women of God should keep close to their hearts.
As you mature in Christ, you will be able to distinguish the
people and environments that are not positive or edifying. It
can be challenging to deal with negative people, situations,
and environments. You may be tempted to think: *This is just
the way things are. Things will never change.* Wait, you do
have a choice in deciding who is in your circle of influence.
God has equipped you with the power to choose associations
that honor Him.

This means you don't have to constantly subject yourself to
people who hurt your feelings, who make you feel bad about
yourself, who do things that are against the Word of God,
or who do things that would lead you to sin. You may not
change the attitudes and behaviors of those around you, but
you can *change* the people with whom you associate. As you
mature in Christ, it will be necessary to let certain people and

14

certain behaviors go. Why? Because Jesus Christ wants you to have an abundant life, not one filled with constant chaos, drama, and pain. Whereas Christ is the Prince of Peace, Satan is the author of confusion.

When you decide to separate from old influences, others may get upset. This is okay. Pray for them and move forward. You can't go wrong by following Jesus Christ, but you can take the wrong path by following negative people. The more you choose to honor God with your life and associations, the more peace, happiness, and joy you will have. Your spiritual walk with Christ will be made stronger when you choose a Godly circle of influence.

Health: Eat more greenery. Salads are a healthy way to add essential vitamins to your diet. They promote healthy weight management.

Emotions: Join a church or community group with like-minded individuals who share your faith and interests. You may find that you have many other interests in common. If possible, discuss ways you can use your faith to impact your work environment or your community in a positive way.

Prayer: Dear Father, I thank you for helping me to recognize negative influences in my life. Help me to separate from people and environments that prevent me from honoring you with my life. I repent for any areas of disobedience in my life. Help me to submit my life to you in all things. In Jesus' name, Amen.

Inspirational Song: "Have Your Way" by Deitrick Haddon

Day Eight

ANGER: A POWERFUL AND DANGEROUS EMOTION

He who is slow to anger is better than the mighty,
And he who rules his spirit, than he who captures a city.

Proverbs 16:32

Spirit: *H*ave you ever lashed out in anger? Have you ever sent a damaging text message or email to someone who offended you? Have you ever given a glaring look of disapproval to someone who *stepped on your toes*? If you have, you are not alone. All of God's children are imperfect people who sometimes say and do the wrong things, especially when they are angry.

Anger is a powerful emotion. If left unchecked, it can become dangerous. It can lead you to sin. God encourages us to "cease from anger and forsake wrath because it only leads to evil doing" (Psalm 37:8). Anger can lead you to respond to challenging people and situations in a negative way. Being angry on your job will cause you to confront co-workers or those in leadership in a hostile way. Being angry at home will lead you to constantly gripe, fuss, and complain about your spouse, children, and other family members. As a member of the body of Christ, anger prevents you from working with others to build up God's kingdom.

Anger has its consequences. For example, many beautiful, dynamic, and powerful women of God are sitting in prison because they *snapped* over something that made them angry. They didn't manage their emotions in a healthy way. Although God can still use them, they are dealing with the repercussions of their actions. You have the power to choose how you will respond to challenging people and situations. As a woman of God, you are called to be a light in the world (Matthew 5:14). You are called to exemplify the fruit of the Spirit in your daily walk with Christ. Galatians 5:22-23 lists the fruit of the Spirit or characteristics that Christians should exemplify. They include love, joy, peace, longsuffering, kindness, goodness, faithfulness, gentleness, and self-control. Learn to manage your anger in a healthy way. Otherwise, your anger will manage you, and lead you to make decisions that have negative consequences.

Health: Stress leads to anger. In turn, anger can have a negative impact on your health. It can cause migraines/tension headaches, ulcers, and acid reflux. It can also lead you to have a heart attack. To ensure that you maintain optimal health, engage in activities that will help you de-stress and relax such as writing, cooking, singing, dancing, or bicycling.

Emotions: If you struggle with managing your anger, subscribe to free online tutorials related to anger management and relaxation. YouTube.com offers many helpful tutorials on a variety of subjects. If you need additional assistance with managing your anger, seek out local counseling services. Your church may even offer these services.

Prayer: Dear Father, help me to process my anger in a healthy way. Let your Holy Spirit guard my thoughts, actions, and emotions every day. Let me always seek to honor you. In Jesus' name, Amen.

Inspirational Song: "Perfect Peace" by Marvin Sapp

Day Nine

DOING YOUR BEST

In the same way, let your light shine before others,
So that they may see your good works and give glory to your
Father who is in heaven.

Matthew 5:16

Spirit: Unexpected blessings come when you do your best unto the Lord. You may feel unprepared, inadequate, or inferior in comparison to others, but God does not see you that way. He simply wants you to do your very best unto Him and in service to Him. As His child, you are pre-equipped with all you need to be successful in life.

Doing your best unto the Lord requires a strong level of trust in Him. He also requires devotion (e.g., prayer, reading the bible, worship, and being a faithful steward) to Him in your daily walk. Above all, He desires you to hone your God-given skills and use them in a way that honors Him and draws others unto Him.

When you are asked to lead on the job, in your home, at church, at school, or in the community, God does not expect you to be perfect. No, He simply expects your very best. This means doing the best work that is required of you, in the most effective way, and in a way that benefits Him and pleases others. When you commit your best work unto the Lord, He gets the glory, and through your service, others are drawn to Him.

Health: Pay close attention to what you are drinking each day. Poor drink choices can impact your productivity. Drinking water will help you keep a clear mind and stay hydrated. It also stimulates your metabolism. Having a clear mind and a boost of energy will help you perform your very best work throughout each day.

Emotions: You can't do your best unto the Lord if you trying to be Superwoman. If you are juggling too many responsibilities, you will become overwhelmed in no time. Pay special attention to the area of your life that is most stressful or demanding. Write a short list of your daily tasks. On a second list, write down ways you can eliminate the most stressful tasks. Delegate responsibility to other trustworthy individuals. Focus on one or two things that you do best. Then, use your energy to glorify God while cultivating those special areas.

Prayer: Dear Father, I thank you for the gifts and talents you have given me. Help me to walk in wisdom and make the best use of your blessings in my life. When I feel ill-equipped, insecure, and discouraged about my ability to perform a task, help me to see myself through your eyes: the eyes of love. Equip me with the confidence to perform tasks in an efficient way. Remove pride and selfishness from my heart and give me humble spirit to do any task required of me, especially tasks that benefit your people and uplift your Kingdom. In Jesus' name, Amen.

Inspirational Song: "Well Done" by Deitrick Haddon

Day Ten

GOD: YOUR BIGGEST CHEERLEADER

What shall we then say to these things?
If God be for us, who can be against us?

Romans 8:31

Spirit: Have you ever been excited about a new opportunity to grow personally or professionally? Were you eager to share your *good news* with someone close to you? Did that person reject your good news, offer a snide comment, blow you off, or act resentful of your good fortune? Did it make you feel bad about God's blessings in your life?

This is not uncommon in the life of the believer. It even happened to Joseph, who was favored by his father. His own brothers betrayed him and left him for dead, but God used his pain for good. Sadly, those closest to us have the power to disappoint us the most. When God pours blessings into your life, you will have support from friends, family, church members, co-workers, and even strangers. Similarly, your blessings can make those closest to you and even perfect strangers feel envy, jealously, and resentment. The experience of having supporters turn against you can be painful. Be encouraged: God has you in the palm of His hand.

Why does this occur in the life of the believer? Satan is the culprit. He walks the earth like a roaring lion, seeking those whom he may devour (1 Peter 5:8). As a master manipulator, Satan convinces others that they are somehow missing out on God's blessings. In turn, their admiration of your spiritual gifts evolves into frustration when they compare your perceived success to their own success. Their frustration evolves into envy of your blessings or perceived success. Their envy evolves into spite and they begin to mistreat you. Spite evolves into jealously. Jealously evolves into full-blown hatred. Despite the tools of the enemy, God promises that, "No weapon formed against you shall prosper" (Isaiah 54:17).

As a woman of God, you can't spend your time worrying about those who may not approve of God's blessings in your life. Their resentful attitudes emanate from a lack of spiritual growth, a lack of trust in God, and a lack of knowledge of God's word. In many instances, outsiders can only see God's glory in your life. They may not be aware of the extreme sacrifice or tribulations you had to walk through to receive God's blessings.

If you are walking through a season when those closest to you have withdrawn their support of you, remain prayerful, but also thankful. Thank Him for your blessings. Thank Him for your supporters. Though it may be difficult, be humble enough to pray for those who may have displaced feelings toward you. Keep looking to God. He's your biggest cheerleader. In the end, He'll turn the pain of rejection into a blessing in your life.

Health: Learning how to remove yourself from toxic environments can positively impact your health. When people engage in gossip or behavior that makes you uncomfortable, have the courage to refuse to listen. You may even be required to walk away from certain people and situations, especially if they are hostile interactions. Your health is important. Dealing with stress, drama, and negativity will only make you sick. Those things are not a part of God's plan for your life. Learn to walk away.

Emotions: As a woman of God, you may have a tendency to analyze a situation from every angle. This is helpful when it comes to serving the Kingdom and doing edifying work for the Lord. However, when it comes to trying to figure out why people have negative intentions toward you, overanalyzing things can be harmful. Learn to accept that you are God's child and He loves you unconditionally. Everyone will not like you. Everyone will not cheer you on. Choose to focus on the positive people in your life. Don't waste your energy analyzing the negative motives of others.

Prayer: Dear Father, I thank you for the support team you have placed in my life. Help me to walk tall. Keep me centered on doing your Holy will. In Jesus' name, Amen.

Inspirational Song: "If God Be For Us" by Three Winans Brothers

Day Eleven

DEALING WITH INSECURITY

I will praise thee; for I am fearfully and wonderfully made:
marvelous are thy works; and that my soul knoweth right well.

Psalm 139:14

Spirit: God made you and He loves you. It does not matter if you have acne, need to lose a few pounds, have wrinkles, or have an imperfect smile. Nothing can ever change God's love for you. You are His child. The world may pressure you to have the "perfect" physical features to be accepted by the masses. Friends may reject you if you don't look the part. Family may criticize your imperfections. Don't put too much weight into what others say about you. Instead, let the Word of God reveal to you the truth about what God says about you.

God's standards of acceptance are completely different than the world's. People say, "Come unto us, but only if you have possessions, beauty, and popularity." God says, "Come unto me as you are." Trying to meet the world's standards can be highly frustrating. Doing so can lead you to develop low self-esteem, become depressed, and even suicidal. Remember, as God's heir, you are called to be confident and strong, and to have faith in God Almighty. You are called to live and not die!

Reject the pressure to fit the world's standard. Don't try to fit in when you are called to stand out. It is wise for you to begin to see yourself as the apple of God's eye: a woman who is fearfully and wonderfully made. God is perfect. His love is perfect. He made you in His own image. Let this powerful knowledge always remind you just how special you are to God.

Health: If there's an area of your life you wish to change, you have the power to do so. Sometimes physical changes are needed for our personal growth. Don't be afraid to do the things that will benefit your health. If your doctor has *strongly* recommended a surgery that could improve or even save your life, don't delay it. Take action and always remain proactive about your health. What you put off today could impact you in a negative way, tomorrow.

Emotions: Don't play into the media images. Many women develop eating disorders when they try to emulate their favorite celebrity. It's perfectly normal to admire things that others do or to be inspired by others. Identify and associate with friends and networks of people who are positive, uplifting, and inspiring. Surround yourself with people who inspire you to be your very best in a healthy way.

Prayer: Dear Father, I thank you for making me in your image. When I feel insecure or self-conscious, or compare myself to others, help me understand how abundant your love is toward me. Bless my associations and friendships. Put healthy, positive people in my circle of influence. Remove any negative person or ungodly force from my life. Let me always look to your standards as the measuring stick for how I live my life and view myself. In Jesus' name, Amen.

Inspirational Song: "I Am Not Alone" by Kari Jobe

Day Twelve

COPING WITH A BROKEN HEART

He healeth the broken in heart, and bindeth up their wounds.

Psalm 147:3

Spirit: Heartache can come from a difficult breakup with a boyfriend, divorce from your spouse, the death or sickness of a child or parent, family turmoil, separation from friends, and unfilled desires. Heartache can be long lasting and difficult to overcome. It can deprive you of mental clarity and rob your sense of peace. Heartache can influence wrong thinking about yourself and others. When you are in a pit of despair, feeling lonely, and dealing with a broken heart, it is important to keep a faith-centered perspective. God has given you His Word. Use it as a tool to provide wisdom and strength as you deal with heartache. It will help you process your concerns in a healthy way.

As you deal with heartache, you may not feel like praying or reading your Bible. You may simply want to be alone, isolated from the world, and cry. You may not even have an appetite for food. It is important to remember His promise to be strength to the broken hearted and to bind up their wounds (Psalm 147:3). God also promises to never leave nor forsake you (Hebrews 13:5)

Because God is omniscient, He knows everything. In other words, God Almighty knows about the pain you are experiencing. He knows about your restless nights. He knows every time you pace the floor in worry or grief. He knows when you cry yourself to sleep. He knows that you may not understand why you are experiencing heartache. Most important, He cares about every single thing you are experiencing.

God did not promise that you would not have pain and heartache. Jesus experienced the pain of the Cross, separation from his loved ones, and the separation from His Father. Yet, Jesus kept faith in God. Even at the Cross while anguishing in pain, Jesus held fast to God's promise to use His suffering for good (Romans 8:28). Indeed, He did.

Today may be challenging. It may be difficult for you to get out of bed. Your heartache may be unbearable. If you will keep the faith and try to focus on the goodness of God amidst your struggle, God will use your pain for good. Your testimony will one day bless someone who needs prayer, encouragement, and a listening ear.

Health: Engage in 45 minutes of exercise each day this week. Exercising will help you deal with your feelings and emotions in a healthy way.

Emotions: When you are dealing with heartbreak, your hobbies or favorite pastimes will be essential to explore. Focus on things that bring you joy, whether that's photography, cooking, writing, dancing, or even visiting the movies. Having an outlet will help you take your mind off your present situation.

Prayer: Dear Father, heartbreak is a part of life. You didn't promise that my life would be easy, but you did promise to be near to me during difficult times. I pray for your strength and guidance as I cope with this painful situation. In Jesus' name, Amen.

Inspirational Song: "Yesterday" by Mary Mary

Day Thirteen

MEDITATING ON GOD'S WORD

*But his delight is in the law of the LORD; and in his law doth
he meditate day and night.*

Psalm 1:2

Spirit: *You* live in a world that can assault your peace
of mind on a daily basis. Most busy women find themselves
overwhelmed and stressed by the reality of their lives. You
may experience stress from your daily commute to and
from work. Or, you may have to meet demanding business
deadlines. Typically, busy women may not release stress in
the healthiest way. Unreleased stress can lead to various health
problems such as high-blood pressure, migraine headaches,
depression, stomachaches, and fatigue.

There are many ways to alleviate stress. One way is
meditating on God's word. It involves deep introspection
and focus while reading God's Word. When you read God's
Word, you will find that some passages of scripture speak to
your specific situation. Meditate on that scripture or passage.
Ask God to show you how to apply the passage to your life
or your unique situation.

A helpful way to meditate on God's Word is to set the
atmosphere in your home or office. You can do so by
burning incense and/or a scented candle. You can also set the

atmosphere by listening to your favorite inspirational music. When meditating, you should seek to eliminate distractions, find a place of inner peace, and communicate with God.

Meditating on God's Word can be relaxing, refreshing, and renewing. It can help you alleviate stress and anxiety. It is a practice that will benefit you and your whole family.

Health: Take a 20 minute walk today. Take a moment away from your work project and walk outside. Rest in His presence and enjoy God's beautiful world.

Emotions: Visit a local Christian bookstore. Purchase a book of God's Promises to read. Promise books can be used as a quick reference to help you keep the Word of God close to your heart.

Prayer: Dear Father, it is important for me to honor you with my time. Direct my path and show me ways to rearrange my schedule so that I honor you each and every day by reading your precious Word. In Jesus' name, Amen.

Inspirational Song: "Ultimate Relationship" by Donald Lawrence and the Tri-City Singers

Day Fourteen

DEALING WITH LIFE'S CURVEBALLS

But they that wait upon the Lord shall renew their strength;
they shall mount up with wings as eagles; they shall run,
and not be weary; and they shall walk, and not faint.

Isaiah 40:31

Spirit: *In* life, you may be knocked down by unexpected circumstances and situations, such as the death of a loved one, the sudden end of a relationship, loss of job security, or an unexpected bill, etc. Life has a way of throwing you curveballs. Sometimes you may face two or three unexpected situations that try your faith. As believers, we are challenged to, "Count it all joy, knowing that trials and tribulations of this life worketh patience" (James 1:2-3). Yes, trials can be painful. Sometimes, your trials may not make sense. Remember, God did not say you would not face trials in this life. He did say He would send you a Comforter during your time of trouble (John 14:16). When life throws you unexpected curveballs, don't focus on what you have lost. Instead, count the many blessings that you still enjoy (e.g., family, friends, talents, and the ability to give thanks).

Step out on faith and believe God will see you through the situation you are facing. Whether the challenge you are facing is a dim health prognosis for you or a loved one, a dire financial situation, or a broken heart, believe God to be *big* in your situation. Trust Him to prove Himself strong. God can do anything but fail. When you feel down and despondent about your situation, find a reason to praise God. Better yet, sow a seed into the lives of other people. Sometimes, the best way to cope with your problems is to help other people with their problems. Curveballs will come. They will be fast, powerful, and unexpected. By keeping God first, you'll be able to remain steadfast and in good faith while under pressure.

Health: Soup is comfort food. However, some store versions are filled with sodium. Take time to create a healthy, low-sodium version of your favorite soup. Soup is food for the soul.

Emotions: The Word of God encourages you to: "Speak to yourself in psalms and hymns and spiritual songs, singing and making melody in your heart to the Lord" (Ephesians 5:19). Create an inspirational mantra to repeat to yourself when you feel overwhelmed by trials such as: "I am powerful. I am strong. I am a child of God. I will get through this."

Prayer: Dear Father, you know my needs. You know my feelings about the curveball that has been thrown at me. Give me a persevering spirit. Help me to keep my eyes focused on you as I face this unexpected challenge. In Jesus' name, Amen.

Inspirational Song: "Encourage Yourself" by Donald Lawrence and the Tri-City Singers

Day Fifteen

THE BENEFIT OF FORGIVENESS

And when ye stand praying, forgive, if ye have ought
against any: that your Father also which is in heaven may
forgive you your trespasses.

Mark 11:25

Spirit: Forgiveness benefits you more than it benefits
the person who offended you. There will be numerous
opportunities for you to live in offense. It takes more effort
to remain upset about an offense than it does to forgive
the offender. Sometimes it is difficult to forgive, but God
commands you to forgive, to love, and to move forward with
your life.

In some instances, the offender may be aware of the offense
but unwilling to address it. This can cause you to feel
extremely frustrated and disappointed. In other instances, the
offender might be unaware that they have hurt you in some
way. Whether the offender apologizes to you or not, make a
conscious decision to forgive and move forward with your
life. Why? The answer is simple: Unforgiveness causes you to
harbor bitterness in your heart. When your heart is hardened
by bitterness, it is hard to let love in. Practicing forgiveness
can be hard. As with anything else in life, the more you
practice something, the more skilled you will become.

If you are still not convinced that you should forgive and forgive today, think of the many things you have asked God to forgive you for. Ask yourself this question: If God shared my same attitude and beliefs about forgiveness, would my sins be forgiven? Choose to forgive because God has forgiven you.

Health: Make an effort to read the nutritional label and/or nutritional menu on the food you eat this week. Some food items and beverages can be filled with unhealthy fat, sodium, and sugar. Opt for food items and beverages that are healthy.

Emotions: Has someone fallen out of your good graces? Have you held on to hurts from 5, 10, and 15 years ago? Spiritual maturity involves letting go of past offenses. You can't move forward in your life if you are holding on to the past.

Prayer: Dear Father, your love is so powerful. It is more powerful that I can comprehend. Help me to grow in the knowledge of your love. Give me a forgiving spirit. In Jesus' name, Amen.

Inspirational Song: "Jesus, I Want You" by Chante Moore

Day Sixteen

LIVING A DISCIPLINED LIFE

*And Samuel said, Hath the L*ORD *as great delight in burnt offerings and sacrifices, as in obeying the voice of the* LORD*? Behold, to obey is better than sacrifice, and to hearken than the fat of rams.*

I Samuel 15:22

Spirit: The Word of God commands you to walk in obedience to God. No Christian is perfect, however. It was Paul who said, "I do the things that I do not want to do." Living an undisciplined life will always impact you in a negative way. If you are undisciplined with your finances, you may overspend and accrue debt. If you are undisciplined on your job (e.g., being late or taking your position for granted), it can lead to you being terminated. If you are undisciplined with prioritizing your marriage, it can lead to infidelity, separation, and other issues. If you are undisciplined with your health, you may face serious health issues.

God gives you free will. He also gives you the Word to serve as your daily guide for living. Make an effort to live in a way that helps you become more effective for God's kingdom. Make an effort to live in obedience to God's word.

Health: Identify areas in your life that need your immediate attention. Sign up for a healthy 30 day challenge, such as the water challenge. It's simple. Each day, you aim to drink one gallon of water. Pinterest.com has many fun health challenges. Once you commit to something for 30 days, it is likelier to become a habit. Please consult your doctor before making any dietary changes.

Emotions: Learn to not respond to communication right away. Give yourself time to think things through, to check your calendar. By doing so, you'll find that you're less committed, less stressed, and in more control of your day-to-day schedule. This will have a positive impact on your emotional health.

Prayer: Dear Father, help me to live a more disciplined life, a life that brings honor and glory to your name. Strengthen me in areas where I am weak. Give me the courage to make improvements in the areas I struggle with. In Jesus' name, Amen.

Inspirational Song: "Changed" by Tramine Hawkins

Day Seventeen

POURING YOUR HEART OUT TO GOD

God is our refuge and strength, a very present help in trouble.
Therefore will not we fear, though the earth be removed, and
though the mountains be carried into the midst of the sea.

Psalm 46:2

Spirit: God knows your heart. He knows your deepest thoughts. He knows what makes you happy. He knows what makes you frustrated. As a woman of God, you are called to have a reverential fear of God. This means you respect God's power and authority in your life. Having a fear of God does not mean you should not go to God with your concerns and frustrations about challenging people and situations.

When you pour your heart out to God about your challenges, He hears you, He listens, and in His own timing, He will respond. You may be tempted to vent your frustrations on social media, to your coworkers or friends. There is nothing wrong with seeking support systems, but have you first poured your heart out to God? Have you sought His wisdom and His word? Have you taken time to listen to God's voice in the matter?

When you're frustrated, it is easy to do or say things you may regret. To avoid doing things that you may later regret, seek God first. Talk to Him before responding and rest in His presence. He may reveal to you areas in your life that can be improved. He may reveal solutions to your problem in scripture. How will you overcome your present challenge if you do not first talk to God?

Health: Register for a local health awareness class. Your hospital, church, or community center may offer free classes. Invite a friend or loved one.

Emotions: It is okay to cry. Crying is a very healthy emotion. Many women feel ashamed to cry because they fear being perceived as *weak,* when others perceive them to be strong. On the other hand, some women cry often and may feel a sense of embarrassment when they do. God made you special. You are wonderful just as you are. You do not need to apologize for being you. If something upsets you, it is okay to feel sad, hurt, or angry, and to cry. If you are happy about something, it is also okay to express tears of joy and excitement. It is better to learn to deal with your emotions in a healthy way than to bottle them in.

Prayer: Dear Father, give me a heart and mind to seek your wisdom each and every day. In Jesus' name, Amen.

Inspirational Song; "Open My Heart to You" by Yolanda Adams

Day Eighteen

NO TURNING BACK

If the Son therefore shall make you free,
ye shall be free indeed.

John 8:36

Spirit: Have you ever felt like returning to a situation or an environment that was not healthy for you? Perhaps you left an abusive relationship or released a bad habit? Maybe you received a good health report and were released from a certain medication, but you don't know how life will be without it. Growing as a person can be challenging. At present, you may not be able to see the awesome future God has in store for you. You may be tempted to hold on to the past.

When you feel you want to revert to an old behavior or return to a situation God has released you from, seek the Word of God. Whom the Son sets free is free indeed. With God's support, you will be able to leave the past in the past. Remember, God desires the best for your life. Once He sets you free from a situation or a person, embrace your freedom and don't look back.

Health: Purge your house of bad foods and unhealthy snacks. Clean out your pantry, cabinets, refrigerator, etc. Make a commitment to purchase healthy snacks.

Emotions: In addition to purging out your home of unhealthy food items, it is also healthy to purge your mind of negative thoughts about those from your past. Search your heart. If you find yourself growing angry or resentful over a person or situation from the past, seek God's wisdom. Ask Him to purge your heart, mind, and spirit of anything that does not bring glory to Him.

Prayer: Dear Father, I thank you for freeing me from my past. Help me to walk confidently in the freedom you have given me. Give me peace of mind and equip me with the strength to never return to a person or environment that does not enrich my life. In Jesus' name, Amen.

Inspirational Song: "I Won't Go Back" by William McDowell

Day Nineteen

THE NECESSITY OF PRAYER

And he withdrew himself into the wilderness, and prayed.

Luke 5:16

Spirit: When God sends you a gentle nudge, listen. Sometimes God will burden your heart with a strong desire to pray, to sow a financial seed, or to give to others in some special way. When God calls you to pray, it is His way of trying to connect with you, to send you a message. Through prayer, God sensitizes you to special situations and gives you direction.

He even uses prayer as a way to prepare you for unforeseen spiritual battles, and/or unforeseen danger. What should you pray for? There are countless people, places, and situations you can pray for. Pray for yourself, your spouse, your children, your parents, your relatives, your pastor and church family, your community, your workplace, your supervisors, your finances, and your health. Pray for your continued spiritual, personal, and emotional growth. Do not forget to include the concerns of others as a priority in your daily prayer life.

Pray for our country's leadership. Pray for those living in the United States and abroad. Pray individually, corporately, and globally. In all you do, pray! The next time you feel God prompting you to pray for a situation, do so. Even if you do not receive a prompting, make prayer a priority in your life. You can never go wrong with prayer.

Health: Instead of reaching for a candy bar, caffeinated beverage, or potato chips, choose a healthy snack at lunch today. Have a piece of fruit, a low fat yogurt, or a handful of healthy nuts like almonds.

Emotions: Kickstart your morning with prayer at home. Praying about situations before you leave home will help you better manage your emotions throughout the day. Set the tone for your day with prayer and inspirational music.

Prayer: Dear Father, thank you for meeting my needs. Help me to make prayer a priority in my life each and every day. In Jesus' name, Amen.

Inspirational Song: "One on One" by Zacardi Cortez

AUTHOR'S SPECIAL REFLECTION

Day Twenty

BLESSED WHILE WAITING

Wait on the Lord: be of good courage,
and he shall strengthen thine heart:
wait, I say, on the Lord.

Psalm 27:14

Spirit: *Your* best friend recently married and another friend calls to say, "I'm having a baby." Although you are excited for them, you find yourself longing, wondering, and secretly asking God, "Lord, when will it be my turn?" What do you do when everyone around you experiences joys such as a great job promotion, a new fiancé, a new home, a new degree, a new car or a new baby? How do you stay focused on God when your life's dreams or goals have not come to fruition? The answer is simple: You wait on the Lord. "Just wait on the Lord" is a phrase that Christians frequently use. Truthfully, after months and years of waiting on a dream or a goal to materialize, "Wait on the Lord" is often the last thing any Christian woman desires to hear. Through my life experiences, I have found that there is a blessing in working hard to achieve my life's goals. I have also discovered the blessing in waiting on God to bring positive things to pass in my life.

The waiting process can be difficult. However, it is important to always remember that you serve a God who knows the plans He has for you (Jeremiah 29:11). He makes no mistakes. If your dating relationship ended, if the business deal did not materialize, and if someone else was hired for the job, you must not lose your faith in God.

In addition to keeping faith in God, it is important to keep believing in yourself and in your dreams. God may have an alternate plan for your life. Or, He may need you to wait for a period of time. There is a blessing in waiting on God to fulfill the desires of your heart. Unfortunately, rushing ahead of His timing or being out of His will can result in extreme frustration and negative consequences for you.

God is a loving Father who desires to protect you from hurt, harm, and danger. A waiting period may be God's way of protecting you from a bad decision that could have disastrous consequences for your life.

Waiting on Your Spouse

If God has not sent you a husband and you have no dating prospects, do not lose heart. The dry season may be God's way of helping you to focus on Him instead of your personal desires. It is important to remember that God's timing is not your timing. The waiting period you are experiencing might be necessary for your spiritual, financial, emotional, and personal growth; therefore, do not be discouraged.

Where's My Blessing?

Instead of asking God, "Where is my blessing or breakthrough?" submit your goals and desires unto the

Lord. Ask Him what He desires to teach you during your season of waiting. Too often, women of God find themselves frustrated and bitter when their goals do not come to pass in the timeframe they imagined.

My Personal Testimony

I experienced the pain of frustration in my life. After college, my life's plan was to attend law school and get married by age 26. I had it all planned out. I was extremely confident that my goals would materialize, but by March of my senior year of college, I knew that law school was not in my immediate future. Having applied to many schools, I was rejected from every school I applied to. I was devastated. I felt that I had let my family down. I let myself down. For weeks, I could not let go of my feelings of insecurity about being rejected from law school. To add salt to my wounded ego, my friends were being accepted into graduate and professional schools of their choice. I was supportive of and genuinely happy for my friends, but I was largely disappointed in myself.

My Pity Party

One day, I called my mother to have a pity party and she frankly, yet lovingly, said, "Stop crying and suck it up." She continued, "Child, you are not a failure. You have done great things with your life and at such a young age. You must remember to always put God first in your plans. Getting rejected from law school is not the end of the world; rejection is a part of life. Your family is proud of you," my mother said, "but you must also remember to have a Plan B if your goals don't materialize." Friends, my mother was absolutely right! I quickly learned that while it is always wise to have a plan in life, it is truly unwise to omit God from the planning.

In All Things, Seek God First

Law school and marriage by age 26 were my goals, but I did not ask God what He desired for my life. I just made the plan and asked God to co-sign on my plan. That was the wrong thing to do. The rejection experience taught me the importance of seeking God's wisdom for decisions, big and small. The experience also taught me humility. It taught me to not trust in my own capabilities and talents. It strengthened my determination to persevere despite the obstacle I faced.

Work On You

The law school rejection led me to self-reflect on areas I needed to improve in. I learned the importance of planning and research. In many instances, we do not succeed because we prepare to fail. We prepare to fail in life by not prioritizing our time, by procrastinating, and by getting sidetracked by people and other goals. I learned that to be successful at any endeavor, I would have to become more focused and disciplined. Sometimes God will use rejection to improve our character.

Failing Again

By age 23, I truly prepared for and decided to reapply to law school. Again, I was rejected. This time, I was not devastated because I knew I had given 100 percent of myself to the application process. I was able to encourage myself by remaining involved in church and the community, finishing a graduate degree, working full-time, and honing my God-given skills and talents in other areas.

Redirection Lead to a Blessing

I did not reapply to law school. By age 25, I had grown stronger in the Lord, was writing more, attending church more frequently, serving in many areas, and felt God changing my heart's desire. I applied to one doctoral program. Not only was I accepted, but I also received a full academic fellowship that covered expenses for a second master's degree and a PhD.

Closed Doors

Today, I praise God for His handiwork in my life. He has blessed me with many professional, academic, and personal opportunities. As I reflect on my life, I now see how God was aligning things in my favor. I now see how my rejection was leading me to a bigger blessing. The waiting was for a reason. When God closed the doors to law school, I was forced to move in accordance with His will for my life.

Discovering Talents

During my waiting period, I was also forced to look introspectively to discover talents which I learned to hone and use for Him while building a professional career for myself. Yes, waiting can be a challenging process, but I have learned that it is much better to relinquish control, wait on God's timing, and trust God to be God.

In closing, if your desire is to have a job, become a parent, purchase a house, get married, obtain a degree, or be used in the ministry, do not lose heart if your goals do not immediately materialize. You will face setbacks in life, but you must not give up. Setbacks are necessary to draw you nearer to God.

God will use your setbacks to strengthen your spirit. They will give voice to your personal testimony. In turn, your personal testimony should be used to bring honor to God and encourage others along the way. Indeed, there is a blessing in waiting.

Health: Download a fun health app and use it to help you reach your fitness goals.

Emotions: Don't hate, congratulate. Support others who have received blessings in their life. The positive energy you share with others will return to you in due season.

Prayer: Dear Father, I thank you for the blessings in my life. Help me to recognize that you are all-powerful and all-knowing. You know what's best for me. I may not like the path I am on today, but I trust that you are working things out for my good. In Jesus' name, Amen.

Inspirational Song: "I Am" by Jason Nelson

Day Twenty-One

PREPARATION FOR THE JOURNEY

*For my thoughts are not your thoughts, neither are your
ways my ways, saith the LORD.
For as the heavens are higher than the earth,
so are my ways higher than your ways,
and my thoughts than your thoughts.*

Isaiah 55:8-9

Spirit: God is all knowing. He knows your today and
your tomorrow. He knows exactly what is best for you. In
life, you will face situations that make you question God's
movement. For example, working a boring job, and working
with difficult people, can try your patience. You may want to
scream: "Lord, I know you have something better for me."
You are right, God does have something better for your life.
Before you throw in the towel and quit your job or behave
ungodly toward someone, consider what God is up to in your
life.

Could it be that the boring job you loathe is actually teaching
you patience and perseverance? Could your experiences
dealing with challenging people be preparing you for ministry
work in your future? Could the heartache and pain you are
experiencing inspire you to write a book, pen an inspirational
song, or share your testimony to a broader audience? You

don't know your future, but God knows. He knows all about you.

God is the ultimate teacher. You may not like His method of instruction now, but by digging deeper and stepping outside your comfort zone, you'll see that God is actually preparing you for the next level of success in your life. Trust Him with your every breath. Seek His face when you don't understand, grow frustrated, or want to quit. The very thing you hate now may be something God uses to bless you with in the future.

Health: If you are struggling with your physical health, seek out a personal trainer or a professional health coach to help you reach your goals. Improving your health may require the assistance and guidance of a trained professional.

Emotions: Check your perspective. Find a way to see the positive outcome in a difficult situation. Is your glass half empty or is it half full? Keeping a positive perspective on life will help you maintain a positive attitude.

Prayer: Dear Father, make me mindful to do all things without grumbling and complaining (Philippians 2:14). In Jesus' name, Amen.

Inspirational Song: "This is My Season" by William Murphy

Day Twenty-Two

KEEP YOUR JOY

For we wrestle not against flesh and blood,
but against principalities, against powers,
against the rulers of the darkness of this world,
against spiritual wickedness in high places.

Ephesians 6:12

Spirit: Some people do not have joy in their lives. They enjoy making other people miserable. The adage goes: "Misery loves company." Satan often uses other people to carry out his plan of attack. Because Satan is the author of confusion, he doesn't want you to have peace in your life (1 Corinthians 14:33). He can use others to cause disruptions in your family, work, and personal life. How do you deal with the people Satan is using to steal your joy? The answer is simple: You confront Satan's attacks with the Word of God.

Determine in your mind and heart that no one will steal your joy. Determine in your mind and heart that no one will destroy your family unit, that no person's actions can force you to quit your job, and that no person has the power to disrupt the peace God has given you. Use the challenging opportunity before you as a way to share God's love with those who may not know Him.

Keep enjoying each day. Always seek to be a blessing to others in action and in deed. By doing so, God will bless your life in ways you never imagined. He will bless you when you relinquish control and let Him fight your battles.

Health: Let it go. Pick and choose your battles. Small disputes with others are not worth the cost to your physical health.

Emotions: Learn positive and professional ways to speak up for yourself. Set boundaries with others. You will have more emotional peace when you speak up for yourself. You will feel more empowered.

Prayer: Dear Father, when I want to retaliate against others, help me to seek your wisdom and guidance. Teach me to step aside, close my mouth, and allow you to fight my battles. In Jesus' name, Amen.

Inspirational Song: "The Battle is Not Yours" by Yolanda Adams

Day Twenty-Three
COMFORTING OTHERS

Greater love hath no man than this,
that a man lay down his life for his friends.

John 15:13

Spirit: God may use you to comfort someone during their time of need. Will you be ready to serve? Supporting a caregiver with words of praise, comforting the grief stricken, praying for a neighbor experiencing financial trials, or making a home cooked meal for a new mother and her family are small ways you can extend love, care, and comfort to others.

It is easy to only look at your circumstances and your needs, but God has called you to do so much more. Has your busy schedule prevented you from reaching out to someone who you know is in need? If so, set aside time in your schedule to make a personal connection with them.

Ask God to reveal to you ways you can help others in need. Make extending comfort to others a family affair. Encourage those in your family unit to help others in need.

Health: Caregiver burden can drain you. If you are caring for others, make an effort to take a daily walk to alleviate stress and to maintain good health.

Emotions: Reach out to a friend who is down on his or her luck. Invite them to a movie. Sharing laughter with a close friend can bring comfort to both of you.

Prayer: Dear Father, use me to bring comfort to those in need. Give me the right words to say and a heart filled with compassion. In Jesus' name, Amen.

Inspirational Song: "Take Me to the King" by Tamela Mann

Day Twenty-Four

ANXIETY: SATAN'S FAVORITE WEAPON

The LORD is my light and my salvation; whom shall I fear?
The LORD is the strength of my life; of whom
shall I be afraid?

Psalm 27:1

Spirit: Satan is real. He is masterful, skillful, and clever. If you are not cautious, you will succumb to anxiety, fear, doubt, and disbelief. As a busy woman, you are probably confronted with constant deadlines, schedules, and duties in multiple areas of your life. At times, you may feel overwhelmed by your responsibilities. This may cause anxiety to overwhelm your heart and spirit.

When you feel stressed and overwhelmed, you should pause and read God's Word. Why? Because Satan likes to convince you that your life is spinning out of control and that your problems are insurmountable. When you feel and think have no sense of control in your life, you will not be able to see God's power in your situation. In turn, you may begin to seek help from unhealthy sources (e.g., harmful relationships, drugs, alcohol) instead of turning to God.

Anxiety robs you of the peace Christ seeks to give. Anxiety leads to insomnia. It impacts your health in a negative way. It also leads you have unhealthy and unrealistic expectations of yourself and others. Unmet expectations lead to frustration. The cycle continues over and over. You are not at your best when you live in a constant state of fear and doubt. Satan uses anxiety and doubt to lead you to think your problems are too big. If he leads you to stop believing in God, he'll lead you to stop believing in yourself. You have so much to offer God's kingdom and this world.

To overcome anxiety, pray and mediate on God's Word. When you draw nearer to God, His calming presence will reassure you that He is in full control.

Health: Take a multivitamin every day. Make this a part of your health regimen.

Emotions: Listen to your favorite sermons each night. Hearing the Word of God before bed will calm your spirit and remind you that God is in full control.

Prayer: Dear Father, help me to remember that you have not given me the spirit of fear, but of power, love, and a sound mind (2 Timothy 1:7). In Jesus name, Amen.

Inspirational Song: "You That I Trust" by the Rance Allen Group

Day Twenty-Five

LOVE EQUALS RESPECT

*There is no fear in love; but perfect love casteth out fear:
because fear hath torment. He that feareth is not made
perfect in love.*

1 John 4:18

Spirit: Whether you're dating, engaged, or married, it is important to know God's view on relationships. His Word is clear: There is no fear in love. This means your intimate partner relationship should be one that brings honor to God and to your life. This also means no other person has the right to bring harm to you in any way.

Unfortunately, many Christian woman silently experience emotional, physical, verbal, and sexual abuse in relationships. They do not speak out because of fear, guilt, shame, and embarrassment. Any relationship that causes you physical, emotional, or psychological abuse is dangerous and unhealthy. God has so much more for your life. You do not have to accept or normalize any form of abuse. Do not let condemnation from others keep you from speaking out or separating yourself from a harmful intimate partner relationship.

You are God's child. You are His handiwork. If He loves you and respects you, shouldn't other people? See yourself through God's eyes. Always believe in yourself. Always know that with Jesus Christ you are not alone. With Jesus, you are always the majority.

Health: Take a self-defense class or a kickboxing class. It's important to know how to protect yourself if you find yourself in a potentially life-threatening situation.

Emotions: Seek immediate help if you are in an abusive relationship. Remember, there is no fear in love.

Prayer: Dear Father, teach me to see myself through your eyes. Help me to free myself from any negative relationship that is not pleasing in your sight. In Jesus' name, Amen.

Inspirational Song: "He Saw the Best in Me" by Marvin Sapp

AUTHOR'S SPECIAL REFLECTION

Day Twenty-Six

WHAT SPIRIT ARE YOU WEARING?

For He had commanded the unclean spirit to come out of the man. For it had often seized him, and he was kept under guard, bound with chains and shackles; and he broke the bonds and was driven by the demons into the wilderness.

Luke 8:29

Spirit: It is ironic how you can detect a person who smokes. They can enter or exit a room and not even have a cigarette burning, but the evidence of their smoking habit follows them. Nicotine smell usually stays on their breath, in their car, in their hair, and in their clothing. You can also detect a smoker by examining their teeth, their lip color, their skin texture, their breathing patterns, and their eye vibrancy. No matter how a smoker may try to conceal his or her habit with cologne, perfume, chewing gum, air freshener, or makeup, the evidence of their habit is unmistakable.

Smoke is not the only thing that can linger on people. In fact, spirits, both negative and positive, can linger on people. Have you ever met someone with a spirit so powerful and commanding that they changed the atmosphere of a room with their presence? I have been in the presence of people who have spirits so positive and vibrant that they caused me to be more optimistic and happy. Similarly, I have been around people with spirits so negative, harsh, and critical that when I was around them, I became uneasy, defensive, and critical.

As a woman of God, you are called to shine God's light in the world (I John 1:5). What influences others to have a negative spirit? Sometimes the answer is complex. Poor personal choices, life experiences, heartache, disappointment, rejection, low self-esteem, depression, and frustration can cause a person to have a negative spirit. A negative spirit has the power to hold us captive and spellbound.

The bible explains the story of the woman with the issue of blood. For 12 years, she dealt with her affliction, but with a touch of the hem of Jesus' garment, she was made whole (Matthew 9:20). Many Christian women of God are like the woman with the issue of blood. For years, they have carried negative spirits with them wherever they go. It is hard for others to see who they really are because they only show their affliction or their negative spirit. For example, instead of others meeting Mary, the kind, compassionate mother of four, they meet Mary, aka Mrs. Bad Attitude. Or, perhaps Ming, the smart, vibrant, jovial college student now comes across as Ming, the Menace to Society, because she has become a depressed, angry, and bitter woman. How would others describe you? What spirit do you wear each day?

Just as God delivered the woman with the issue of the blood from her infirmity, God can deliver you from any stronghold in your life. If a bad spirit has held you spellbound and captive for years, ask God to change you. He is willing to make you brand new. The process will not happen overnight, but if you submit your concerns over to God, He will intervene in a powerful and mighty way.

Health: Sign up for a yoga class. Yoga is very healthy and relaxing. A yoga class can help you focus on what's really important in your life.

Emotions: Stop playing the blame game. Accept responsibility for not having the best attitude and work to change your behavior. You may not be able to change other people or challenging circumstances, but you can choose to change your attitude and outlook.

Prayer: Dear Father, change anything in my life that dishonors you. Help others to see You when they meet me. In Jesus' name. Amen.

Inspirational Song: "Make Me Over Again" by Tonex

Day Twenty-Seven

SURVIVING FAMILY STRIFE

Charity suffereth long, and is kind; charity envieth not; charity vaunteth not itself, is not puffed up; Doth not behave itself unseemly, seeketh not her own, is not easily provoked, thinketh no evil; Rejoiceth not in iniquity, but rejoiceth in the truth; Beareth all things, believeth all things, hopeth all things, endureth all things.

I Corinthians 13: 4-7

Spirit: Strife between parents and children, husband and wives, sisters and brothers originates from one singular source: pride. No one wants to be wrong. Everyone wants their feelings acknowledged and their point of view heard. You may be dealing with strife within your family. The mounting tension within your family may be a source of emotional and physical stress in your life. Although apologies can help to calm the storm, some family issues cannot be resolved with an apology. Some issues are deeper.

During seasons of family conflict and strife, it is important to remember how loving and gracious your Heavenly Father has been to you. God has blessed you with family for a reason. Your family should enrich your life. You should enrich their lives.

Your family will not be perfect. You are not perfect. Still, God can bring good from the imperfections that exist within your family unit. God wants you to love and appreciate the family you have. Learn to recognize positive qualities in your family members. This will help you better understand them and overlook small offenses. Extend love to those within your family as much as you can. Don't let small disputes among family members linger. Resolve disputes quickly. In all you do, strive to live in peace with your family members. They are all you have.

Health: Have a healthy Sunday dinner with your family. Invite them to help you prepare the meal.

Emotions: Learn to walk away. Family conflict can leave you dejected. It can be spiritually, emotionally, and physically draining to remain in an environment where there is family strife. Walking away does not mean you are not willing to heal or acknowledge someone else's point of view. Walking away can be healthy in situations when conflict escalates. Some family conflict is deep-rooted and requires a mediator. Don't stay in environments with those who blatantly disrespect, humiliate, or embarrass you. Go where you're embraced, welcomed, and supported. Follow peace.

Prayer: Dear Father, I submit my family strife unto you. I do not choose to participate. Help me to be a light in my family and a person so shares your love with others. In Jesus' name, Amen.

Inspirational Song: "Jesus at the Center" by Israel and New Breed

Day Twenty-Eight

RISING ABOVE DESPAIR

*We are afflicted in every way, but not crushed; perplexed,
but not despairing; persecuted, but not forsaken; struck
down, but not destroyed.*

2 Corinthians 4:8-9

Spirit: Several years ago, I saw the familiar face of
Bernice King on television. She is the youngest daughter of
civil rights leaders Martin Luther King, Jr. and Coretta Scott
King. Mrs. Coretta Scott King had recently passed. I thought
Bernice was reflecting on the spiritual legacy of her mother.
After a few moments of listening to her, I realized that she
was reflecting on her life and sharing her personal testimony
with the world.

A law student at the age of 23, Bernice was at a low point
in her life. She tried to commit suicide. She stated that a
personal encounter with God led her to put the knife down.
She added, "On the outside, I had it all, but on the inside I felt
that no one loved me or cared about me." I thought Bernice
was brave to share her story. We often assume notable figures
have no problems—that they live *on top of the world*. At the
time, Bernice was not *on top of the world*. In fact, she was at

an all-time low in her life. Since that time, God has used her life in an amazing way. What a powerful testimony.

As a woman of God, you may be able to relate to her testimony. I want to take a moment to explore five important factors that lead Christian women to reach a point of despair in their lives.

Bearing Burdens in Silence

Many women of God shoulder their burdens in silence. They carry burdens that God desires them to relinquish. Each day, they lug their burdens with them to and from home, work, school, and church. They rarely take the time to release their burdens to God. When a woman carries too many burdens, they can paralyze her spiritually, physically, and emotionally. Eventually, she will break. Some burdens are too heavy to bear.

The Pretense of Perfection

Because it is painful to open up and share problems, many women of God have mastered the art of pretending that all is well with the world. The words, "I'm blessed and highly favored," often cover up pain on the inside. Sadly, some women of God pretend with their families, their friends, and with those closest to them. They don't want to share their pain. As such, they walk around smiling their smiles, dressed in their fancy clothes. Outwardly, they appear crisp, cool, and collected, but on the inside, some Christian women are broken, hurt, sick, miserable, unhappy, confused, angry, bitter, tired, sad, depressed, and heart-broken. They are crying out for help; yet, they never say a word. They just pretend well.

Being Everyone's Support System

Unfortunately, many women of God slip into the routine of being everything for everyone else, while being nothing for themselves. They act as a mother to other people's children, while neglecting to nurture their own family bonds. They act as an automatic teller machine (ATM) to their families, friends, and children, while rarely enjoying the fruit of their own labor. They act as a counselor, an advisor, a teacher, and a best friend to those in need. In some cases, the care they give to others is not reciprocated. Being the *solid rock* for everyone else can lead to feelings of despair.

Meeting Other's Expectations

Women of God also try to meet the expectations that others set forth for them. Doing so can lead women to deprioritize God's place in their lives. They may work tirelessly to meet other people's expectations; yet, place God on the back burner of their lives. When God is not first, it leads to a deep sense of spiritual, emotional, and physical imbalance and confusion in a woman's life. Essentially, women of God can have so many *irons in the fire* that they become overwhelmed, frustrated, and hopeless. Hopelessness leads to despair.

An Unbalanced Life

The aforementioned factors all equate to an unbalanced life. An unbalanced life can lead women of God to have a spiritual, physical, and/or emotional breakdown. As a woman of God, you must learn to eliminate behaviors in your life that bring you momentary happiness and garner temporary praise from others, but do not lead to your spiritual, physical, emotional, and personal self-fulfillment.

Sister, I challenge you to value God, your life, your goals, your ambitions, and yourself, first. This does not mean to exist or function selfishly, but it does mean having an awareness that you are not Superwoman. You are not required to meet the standards and expectations of everyone. You are only *required* to meet the standards of God. Because of the grace God freely gives, suicide should never be an option in the life of a believer.

Enjoy your life and take time to breathe, relax and to do things you enjoy. By doing so, you will become more productive in other areas of your life. You will reduce your stress levels and enhance your spiritual, physical, and emotional well-being.

Health: Reduce your sugar intake this week by reading nutrition labels on foods and drinks.

Emotions: Pamper yourself today. Have a manicure, pedicure, or spa day. You deserve it.

Prayer: Dear Father, my life is not my own. Keep me centered and rooted in Your word. Give me Godly confidence to know that suicide will never be an option for my life. In Jesus' name, Amen.

Inspirational Song: "Oceans" by Hillsong United

AUTHOR'S SPECIAL REFLECTION

Day Twenty-Nine

MAKING PEACE WITH OTHERS

If it be possible, as much as lieth in you,
live peaceably with all men.

Romans 12:18

Spirit: *H*ardy Jackson of Biloxi, Mississippi gave voice to the reality of Hurricane Katrina. In a 2005 emotionally charged interview, he told the world how he held onto his wife, Tonetta's hand as flood waters overwhelmed them, loosening their grip with each incoming wave. Of his final moments with his wife, Mr. Jackson said: "And she told me, 'You can't hold me.' She said, 'Take care of the kids. And the grandkids.' Then, she slipped away. That story serves as a reminder of how precious life is.

I am certain Hardy Jackson never imagined he would witness his wife fighting for her life amid raging flood waters. Those same flood waters demolished many cities along the coast and left numerous families displaced and heartbroken. During his final moments with his wife, I doubt Hardy Jackson thought of that argument they probably had over a bill, or that one time Tonetta really made him mad. I doubt he reflected on those bitter words they may have exchanged during the early years of their 20 year marriage, or any disagreement they had the week before Hurricane Katrina. No, I imagine his mind and heart were racing during those final, precious moments with his wife. I image that Mr. Jackson did all he could to hold onto his wife's hand. At the final moment before Tonetta slipped away, I imagine the only thing that mattered to Mr. Jackson was his love for his wife.

Life is Precious

Mr. Jackson died in 2013, but his powerful testimony still has a significant meaning—one that all Christian women can benefit from. The lesson is simple: Life is precious; therefore, treat your loved ones with honor and respect. You do not know when your final day on earth will be. You do not know when your loved ones will pass away.

Settle Petty Differences

As a woman of God, you should work to settle petty differences with others. Do not hold onto grudges, harbor bitterness and anger in your heart, or use your power to bring hurt and/or harm to others. Admitting your mistakes, apologizing or showing compassion or love toward those most significant to you does not make you weak. These many things expose your humanity. The greatest mistake you can make is to allow pride, greed, and selfishness to blight your relationship with others.

Be Open to Forgiving Others

God does not want you to find yourself in a position where you waited too late to apologize, forgive others, or say, "I love you," to someone important in your life. This is why He commands you to be at peace with others. Therefore, make an effort to heal and restore relationships with important people in your life. If someone hurt or betrayed you, forgive that person. If you are being mistreated now, ask God to give you a forgiving spirit and a heart to pray for those who despitefully use you. It is unhealthy to carry hurt, bitterness, or anger another single day, hour, or minute of your life. Forgive today and be at peace with others.

Health: Track the calories in your food this week.

Emotions: Practice patience with others. Engage in a fun activity with your family members. Choose a project that requires team building. This will help you work toward building better communication with each other.

Prayer: Dear Father, help me to settle petty differences with others. In Jesus' name, Amen.

Inspirational Song: "A Heart That Forgives" by Kevin LeVar

AUTHOR'S SPECIAL REFLECTION

Day Thirty

THE PAIN OF YOUR PAST

For I reckon that the sufferings of this present time are not worthy to be compared with the glory which shall be revealed in us.

Romans 8:18

Spirit: Alfonzo Tucker was abandoned by his biological mother, raised by a drug addicted father, and left to survive in a world where he often solved life issues with violence. At the age of 17, after having lived in three different foster homes, Alfonzo was adopted by a loving family. His new family environment allowed him to begin his life again (Tucker, 2003). To walk in his destiny, Alfonzo had to work hard to relinquish the wounds of his past. Today, Alfonzo is a well-established businessman and author of *Noesis: Comprehension and Understanding-The Autobiography of Alfonzo Tucker*. To look at Alfonzo's outward success, you would never know he had a turbulent childhood. Alfonzo had to forgive the wounds of his past in order to embrace the blessings of his future.

Each day, you place your trust and faith in others. You operate with the belief and the expectation that those you trust will act in your best interest. Unfortunately, those who are closest to you, such as your parents, spouse, children, family members, and friends, are often capable of hurting you. They are human. They will make mistakes. As believers, we are commanded to forgive the transgressions of others as Christ has forgiven us (Colossians 3:13). Yet, the act of forgiving a person who was supposed to love, protect, and value you is one of the hardest things to do. Abandonment and abuse can cause you to lose your faith in the inherent good nature of people. When you lose faith, confidence, and trust in others, you can become cynical, defensive, bitter, angry, malicious, unforgiving, guarded, and incapable of allowing love into your heart. Wounds from the past can make you feel devalued, unappreciated, unloved, and disrespected.

You may be like Alfonzo, a survivor of a painful, difficult childhood. You may have experienced childhood molestation, abuse, abandonment, neglect, food insecurity, rape, and poverty. Ignoring your pain and sweeping past issues under the rug is not healthy. If you do not heal the wounds of your past, you will not live at peace in your future. You will not be able to grow spiritually, physically, or emotionally. You will not be able to receive the many blessings God has in store for your life.

Friend, you may be asking: How do I forgive the wounds of the past? How do I remove the hurt in my life and begin living again? How do I reconcile my emotions? How do I release the feelings for anger, betrayal, confusion, and grief? How do I continuously look to God when I am completely broken on the inside?

The answer is simple: You trust God. God knows all about you. He created you. He knows exactly how you feel. He knows that you are tired of carrying those burdens with you. He wants to give you freedom and victory over your past. If you allow Him to heal your pain, He will give you a testimony that helps others along the way.

Start your healing process today by first making peace with God. When bad things happen in your life, it is easy to get mad at God. Understand that God loves you as His own. Being mad at God won't erase the pain of your past, but it will keep you from healing. Talk to God. Let Him know how you feel. Seek His word. There, you will find comfort. When you give your burdens over to God, He will reveal to you His purpose. He will show you that He was walking with you all along.

When you've made peace with God, make peace with yourself. It's easy to blame God for the things that happened to you, but it is also easy to blame yourself. If someone took advantage of you, that is not your fault. Stop blaming yourself. Forgive yourself for things that were beyond your control.

Finally, forgive your offender. As Jesus hung on the Cross, He cried out to God, "Forgive them, Father, for they know not what they do" (Luke 23:34). If Jesus could pray for and forgive those who nailed Him to the Cross, you can pray for those who have offended you.

Healing will set you free. Living in the past, holding onto the past, and being angry over the past will keep you in bondage.

You may have experienced unjust treatment in your past, but God has ordered your steps today. He wants you to be free from your past. Seek Him. Trust Him. Believe Him and know that He can use the painful experiences from your past as a testimony that honors and glorifies His name on earth.

Health: Have you visited the dentist lately? Maintaining good dental health is vital to your overall health.

Emotions: Clean your home or personal environment. Emotional peace is directly tied to your living space. As you work to eliminate negativity from your life, eliminate excess items from your home. You'll find more peace and happiness when you are in a home environment that is clutter free.

Prayer: Dear Father, I can't change my past. I do not want my past to hold me captive. Give me a heart that can forgive others. In Jesus' name, Amen.

Inspirational Song: "Withholding Nothing Medley" by William McDowell

AUTHOR'S SPECIAL REFLECTION

Day Thirty - One

WALK IN YOUR OWN SHOES

Having then gifts differing according to the grace that is given to us, whether prophecy, let us prophesy according to the proportion of faith.

Romans 12:6

Spirit: Beautiful and intelligent, my older sister, Kanika, was always a skilled athlete. Sports being her forte, she played basketball, tennis, softball, flag-football, and ran track throughout her high school years. She has a well-rounded, genuine, and friendly personality which naturally attracts people to her. Growing up, I always admired her talents and friendly disposition. I endeavored to be just like my big sister.

During my pre-teen years, extended family members commented on the differences between my sister and me. Some would say, "You two are like 'night and day' in terms of your personalities, your athletic capabilities, and your different appearances." My parents have always encouraged my sister and me to be individuals. They have encouraged us to be the exact people God created us to be. Succumbing to the "night and day" comments, I decided that I would make an effort to become more like my sister. Thus, I decided to try out for the junior varsity basketball team.

It never occurred to me that I should learn the rules of the game or even practice basketball, I simply showed up at junior-varsity try-outs thinking: *Surely, the apple does not fall too far from the tree.* Pretending that I knew how to play basketball, I mimicked the actions of the rest of the team. When they ran, I ran. When they maneuvered left, I maneuvered left. It was not until the coach separated the team that my inability to play basketball was exposed.

Surrounded by on-lookers and standing in the center of the court, the coach yelled to me: "Collins, take the ball out!" Confused, my mind began to race with questions about the game: *Take the ball* out? *What does take the ball out mean? Where do I take the ball? Outside?* Slightly irritated, the coach yelled again: "Collins, take the ball out!"

The coach's yelling startled me. I immediately proceeded to do as I was instructed. With the ball in my hands, I immediately walked off the basketball court and headed toward the gymnasium's exit. The spectators looked at me with blank and confused stares. Clueless about the game, I did not know the coach wanted me to pass the ball to another player. I naively thought he wanted me to take the ball *outside* the gymnasium.

Exasperated, he screamed: "Collins, what are you doing? Where are you going with the basketball? Get off the court! I thought you knew how to play basketball!" Embarrassed, but also profoundly amused, I exited the basketball court. That was the first and the last time I tried to play basketball. That was the last time I tried to be someone else.

That incident taught me a lot about myself. I learned that God made me unique for a specific reason. Once I realized that I, too, had special talents and gifts, I was able to hone them. I discovered my niche for writing and public speaking. I have been maximizing my God-given talents ever since.

I thought that by walking in my sister's shoes, I would find happiness. However, I soon realized that I could only be me. Yes, I would love to possess a deep knowledge of sports and have a more outgoing personality like my big sister, but I can only walk in my *own* shoes. I doubt that I will ever play sports. I am certain that I will always be slightly introverted. Nevertheless, I am comfortable with who I am and confident that God made no mistakes when He created me (Jeremiah 1:5).

Are You Comfortable in Your Own Shoes?

Friends, I charge you to examine your own life. Are you comfortable in your own shoes or are you attempting to walk in another person's shoes? You may not be moving forward in your life because you are walking in shoes that God has not designed for your feet. You are trying to be everyone else instead of being the individual God has called you to be.

You may long for the talents, gifts, and skills that others possess. If you do not focus on cultivating the gifts God has given you, you will become consumed with trying to attain the anointing that God has placed on another person's life.

You will fail to recognize your own special anointing and calling in life.

Jealousy Stagnates God's Blessings

When you focus on blessings God has given others, you can become jealous and envious of them. To allow jealously and envy to consume you would mean that you fail to recognize that God is "no respecter of persons" (Acts 10:34). Friends, when the spirit of jealously takes root in your life, you deny yourself access to God's bountiful blessings. Jealously is a stronghold. It will consume you and keep you stagnant in every area of your life.

Hoarding Your Spiritual Gifts

Jealously stagnates your progress. A stubborn spirit can do the same. When you become fixated on becoming what you want to become, you will not see the purpose of using your talents to serve God's kingdom. You will hoard your talents and only use them in a way that benefits you and advances your personal agenda. When you hoard your talents and refuse to use them for God's glory, you give Him an ultimatum: "If I can't serve you in my own way, I will not serve you at all." If you do not use your gifts and talents to serve Him, He has the power to take them from you. The choice is yours to make.

Check Your Motives for Serving

As a Christian woman, you must be appreciative of your God-given gifts and talents. You must be willing to let God take control of your life (James 4:10). By trying to walk in another person's shoes and by hoarding your talents, you will miss the opportunity to let God work through you. You will miss the opportunity to bless the lives of others (Acts 20:35).

Moreover, as a woman of God, you have to know your true motives for serving God. Are you seeking praise, acceptance, and notoriety from others, or do you seek to glorify God with your talents (Luke 9:23). God expects you to be patient and to seek His vision for your life. God expects us to be faithful to His vision and to trust that He will do "exceedingly, abundantly, above all that we could ask or think, according to the power that worketh in us" (Ephesians 3:20).

Do Not Despise Small Beginnings

As a steward of Christ, do not despise humble beginnings (Job 8:7). Rather, remain humble and keep a heart that is willing to be used by God on platforms both small and large (1 Peter 5:6).

Your God-given gifts and talents are your ministry (Colossians 4:17). When God calls you to use the talents He has given you, be willing to carry out His purpose. Do not complain because you do not possess the same gifts as others; instead, use what you have to bring honor to His kingdom (Revelation 4:11).

God: No Respecter of Persons

God is no respecter of persons. He has given everyone a gift. Your gift is your ministry. Share it with the world. You have a choice to make. You can choose to stuff your feet in shoes that belong to other people, carry around the weight of jealously and hoard your talents. Or, you can choose to boldly wear your own perfect, unique, God-crafted shoes, and use your unique gifts to inspire the rest of the world. The choice is yours to make!

Sister, I encourage you to step out and wear your own shoes. Start using your unique talents to carry out your God-given purpose. Let go of the notion that you have to be who others expect you to be. Instead, seek to be who Christ wants you to be. Do what He has called you to do. Press into God and trust that in due season, He will show you how to use your talents in a way that brings happiness to you and fulfills His purpose for your life.

Health: Challenge yourself to pick up a new health-related activity. If you have always wanted to learn how to jump rope, ride a bike, jog or run, do so today. Invite a friend to partner with you.

Emotions: Don't make important decisions when you are hungry, angry, lonely and tired (HALT).

Prayer: Dear Father, help me to accept myself as you made me. Help me to walk in my own shoes. In Jesus' name, Amen.

Inspirational Song: "Worth" by Anthony Brown and Group Therapy

The SHE Devotional: 31 Daily Inspirations for a Woman's Spirit, Health and Emotions

Day	Theme	Primary Scripture	Inspirational Song
One	When You Are Tired	2 Corinthians 12:9	"I Need You Now" by Smokie Norful
Two	Experiencing Joy	Nehemiah 8:10	"I Smile" by Kirk Franklin
Three	Forgiving Others	Matthew 6:14-15	"Let Go" by DeWayne Woods
Four	Dedication	Philippians 3:13-14	"I Believe I Can Fly" by Yolanda Adams
Five	Managing Your Priorities	Matthew 6:33	"For Your Glory" by Tasha Cobbs
Six	Making Positive Changes	Luke 9:23	"He Wants It All" by Forever Young
Seven	Your Circle of Influence	Romans 12:2	"Have Your Way" by Deitrick Haddon
Eight	Anger: A Powerful and Dangerous Emotion	Proverbs 16:32	"Perfect Peace" by Marvin Sapp
Nine	Doing Your Best	Matthew 5:16	"Well Done" by Deitrick Haddon
Ten	God: Your Biggest Cheerleader	Romans 8:31	"If God Be For Us" by Three Winans Brothers

Eleven	Dealing with Insecurity	Psalm 139:14	"I Am Not Alone" by Kari Jobe
Twelve	Coping with a Broken Heart	Psalm 147:3	"Yesterday" by Mary Mary
Thirteen	Meditating on God's Word	Psalm 1:2	"Ultimate Relationship" by Donald Lawrence and the Tri-City Singers
Fourteen	Dealing with Life's Curveballs	Isaiah 40:31	"Encourage Yourself" by Donald Lawrence and the Tri-City Singers
Fifteen	The Benefit of Forgiveness	Mark 11:25	"Jesus, I Want You" by Chante Moore
Sixteen	Living a Disciplined Life	I Samuel 15:22	"Changed" by Tramine Hawkins
Seventeen	Pouring Your Heart Out to God	Psalm 46:2	"Open My Heart to You" by Yolanda Adams
Eighteen	No Turning Back	John 8:36	"I Won't Go Back" by William McDowell
Nineteen	The Necessity of Prayer	Luke 5:16	"One on One" Zacardi Cortez
Twenty	Blessed While Waiting	Psalm 27:14	"I Am" by Justin Nelson
Twenty-One	Preparation For The Journey	Isaiah 55:8-9	"This is My Season" by William Murphy

Twenty-Two	Keep Your Joy	Ephesians 6:12	"The Battle is Not Yours" by Yolanda Adams
Twenty-Three	Comforting Others	John 15:13	"Take Me to the King" by Tamela Mann
Twenty-Four	Anxiety: Satan's Favorite Weapon	Psalm 27:1	"You That I Trust" by The Rance Allen Group
Twenty-Five	Love Equals Respect	1 John 4:18	"He Saw the Best in Me" by Marvin Sapp
Twenty-Six	What Spirit Are You Wearing?	Luke 8:29	"Give Me a Clean Heart" by Fred Hammond
Twenty-Seven	Surviving Family Strife	I Corinthians 13:4-7	"Jesus at the Center" by Israel and New Breed
Twenty-Eight	Rising Above Despair	2 Corinthians 4:8-9	"Oceans" by Hillsong United
Twenty-Nine	Living In Peace With Others	Romans 12:18	"A Heart That Forgives" by Kevin LeVar
Thirty	The Pain of Your Past	Romans 8:18	"Withholding Nothing Medley" by William McDowell
Thirty-One	Walk In Your Own Shoes	Romans 12:6	"Worth" by Anthony Brown and Group Therapy

A PRAYER OF SALVATION

I hope you have enjoyed reading *The SHE Devotional: 31 Daily Inspirations for a Woman's Spirit, Health and Emotions™.* The book reflects my desire to share my faith in God and belief in Jesus Christ with the world.

In this life, you will experience joy and happiness, and sorrow and pain. I have faced many triumphs and challenges in my life. When I reflect over my life, I can clearly see that God has always been with me. I am so grateful for His love.

Jesus Christ loves you also. He will walk with you, comfort you, lead and guide you, protect you, and never leave nor forsake you. If you have not accepted Jesus into your life, you are missing out on the greatest gift. I invite you to experience the joy, the happiness, and the sense of security that comes from a personal relationship with Christ. Please, pray this prayer:

Dear Father, I come before you today with a repentant heart. Forgive me of my sins. Today, I accept you and your Holy Word into my heart. I confess that Jesus Christ is my Lord and Savior. I believe He died for my sins. From this day forward, I commit my life to following Christ. I will do so until the end of my days. In Jesus' name I pray, Amen.

Prayer Journal

Prayer Journal

_____
_____
_____
_____
_____
_____
_____
_____
_____
_____
_____
_____
_____
_____
_____
_____
_____
_____
_____
_____
_____
_____
_____
_____
_____
_____

Prayer Journal

_____
_____
_____
_____
_____
_____
_____
_____
_____
_____
_____
_____
_____
_____
_____
_____
_____
_____
_____
_____
_____
_____
_____
_____
_____
_____

Prayer Journal

_____
_____
_____
_____
_____
_____
_____
_____
_____
_____
_____
_____
_____
_____
_____
_____
_____
_____
_____
_____
_____
_____
_____
_____

Prayer Journal

_____

_____

_____

_____

_____

_____

_____

_____

_____

_____

_____

_____

_____

_____

_____

_____

_____

_____

_____

_____

_____

_____

_____

Prayer Journal

_____
_____
_____
_____
_____
_____
_____
_____
_____
_____
_____
_____
_____
_____
_____
_____
_____
_____
_____
_____
_____
_____
_____
_____
_____

DR. SHANI K. COLLINS

Prayer Journal

_____

_____

_____

_____

_____

_____

_____

_____

_____

_____

_____

_____

_____

_____

_____

_____

_____

_____

_____

_____

_____

_____

Prayer Journal

_____

_____

_____

_____

_____

_____

_____

_____

_____

_____

_____

_____

_____

_____

_____

_____

_____

_____

_____

_____

_____

_____

Prayer Journal

Prayer Journal

_____

_____

_____

_____

_____

_____

_____

_____

_____

_____

_____

_____

_____

_____

_____

_____

_____

_____

_____

_____

_____

_____

_____

_____

_____

Prayer Journal

_____
_____
_____
_____
_____
_____
_____
_____
_____
_____
_____
_____
_____
_____
_____
_____
_____
_____
_____
_____
_____
_____
_____
_____
_____

Prayer Journal

_____

_____

_____

_____

_____

_____

_____

_____

_____

_____

_____

_____

_____

_____

_____

_____

_____

_____

_____

_____

_____

_____

_____

_____

_____

Prayer Journal

_____

_____

_____

_____

_____

_____

_____

_____

_____

_____

_____

_____

_____

_____

_____

_____

_____

_____

_____

_____

_____

_____

Prayer Journal

Prayer Journal

_____
_____
_____
_____
_____
_____
_____
_____
_____
_____
_____
_____
_____
_____
_____
_____
_____
_____
_____
_____
_____
_____
_____
_____
_____

Prayer Journal

Prayer Journal

_____
_____
_____
_____
_____
_____
_____
_____
_____
_____
_____
_____
_____
_____
_____
_____
_____
_____
_____
_____
_____
_____
_____
_____
_____

Prayer Journal

_____
_____
_____
_____
_____
_____
_____
_____
_____
_____
_____
_____
_____
_____
_____
_____
_____
_____
_____
_____
_____
_____
_____

Prayer Journal

_____
_____
_____
_____
_____
_____
_____
_____
_____
_____
_____
_____
_____
_____
_____
_____
_____
_____
_____
_____
_____
_____

Prayer Journal

_____
_____
_____
_____
_____
_____
_____
_____
_____
_____
_____
_____
_____
_____
_____
_____
_____
_____
_____
_____
_____
_____
_____
_____
_____
_____
_____
_____

Prayer Journal

_____
_____
_____
_____
_____
_____
_____
_____
_____
_____
_____
_____
_____
_____
_____
_____
_____
_____
_____
_____
_____
_____
_____

Prayer Journal

_____

_____

_____

_____

_____

_____

_____

_____

_____

_____

_____

_____

_____

_____

_____

_____

_____

_____

_____

_____

_____

_____

_____

_____

_____

Prayer Journal

_____

_____

_____

_____

_____

_____

_____

_____

_____

_____

_____

_____

_____

_____

_____

_____

_____

_____

_____

_____

_____

_____

_____

Prayer Journal

_____

_____

_____

_____

_____

_____

_____

_____

_____

_____

_____

_____

_____

_____

_____

_____

_____

_____

_____

_____

_____

_____

_____

_____

_____

_____

Prayer Journal

_____
_____
_____
_____
_____
_____
_____
_____
_____
_____
_____
_____
_____
_____
_____
_____
_____
_____
_____
_____
_____
_____
_____
_____

Prayer Journal

_____
_____
_____
_____
_____
_____
_____
_____
_____
_____
_____
_____
_____
_____
_____
_____
_____
_____
_____
_____
_____
_____

DR. SHANI K. COLLINS

Prayer Journal

_____
_____
_____
_____
_____
_____
_____
_____
_____
_____
_____
_____
_____
_____
_____
_____
_____
_____
_____
_____
_____
_____
_____
_____

Prayer Journal

_____

_____

_____

_____

_____

_____

_____

_____

_____

_____

_____

_____

_____

_____

_____

_____

_____

_____

_____

_____

_____

_____

_____

_____

_____

_____

Prayer Journal

_____

_____

_____

_____

_____

_____

_____

_____

_____

_____

_____

_____

_____

_____

_____

_____

_____

_____

_____

_____

_____

_____

_____

Prayer Journal

_____
_____
_____
_____
_____
_____
_____
_____
_____
_____
_____
_____
_____
_____
_____
_____
_____
_____
_____
_____
_____
_____
_____
_____
_____

Prayer Journal

Prayer Journal

_____
_____
_____
_____
_____
_____
_____
_____
_____
_____
_____
_____
_____
_____
_____
_____
_____
_____
_____
_____
_____

Prayer Journal

_____
_____
_____
_____
_____
_____
_____
_____
_____
_____
_____
_____
_____
_____
_____
_____
_____
_____
_____
_____
_____
_____
_____

Prayer Journal

_____
_____
_____
_____
_____
_____
_____
_____
_____
_____
_____
_____
_____
_____
_____
_____
_____
_____
_____
_____
_____
_____
_____

DR. SHANI K. COLLINS

Prayer Journal

_____
_____
_____
_____
_____
_____
_____
_____
_____
_____
_____
_____
_____
_____
_____
_____
_____
_____
_____
_____
_____
_____
_____

Prayer Journal

_____

_____

_____

_____

_____

_____

_____

_____

_____

_____

_____

_____

_____

_____

_____

_____

_____

_____

_____

_____

_____

_____

_____

_____

Prayer Journal

_____

_____

_____

_____

_____

_____

_____

_____

_____

_____

_____

_____

_____

_____

_____

_____

_____

_____

_____

_____

_____

_____

_____

_____

_____

_____

_____

Prayer Journal

_____

_____

_____

_____

_____

_____

_____

_____

_____

_____

_____

_____

_____

_____

_____

_____

_____

_____

_____

_____

_____

_____

_____

_____

Prayer Journal

_____

_____

_____

_____

_____

_____

_____

_____

_____

_____

_____

_____

_____

_____

_____

_____

_____

_____

_____

_____

_____

_____

_____

Prayer Journal

_____
_____
_____
_____
_____
_____
_____
_____
_____
_____
_____
_____
_____
_____
_____
_____
_____
_____
_____
_____
_____
_____
_____
_____
_____
_____

Prayer Journal

_____

_____

_____

_____

_____

_____

_____

_____

_____

_____

_____

_____

_____

_____

_____

_____

_____

_____

_____

_____

_____

_____

References

Blake, John. (2013, August 25). Moving out of the dreamer's shadow: A King daughter's long journey. *CNN*. Retrieved from http://www.cnn.com/2013/08/25/us/bernice-king-profile/

Corporation, M. (2014, December 12). Hurricane Katrina survivor finds peace as he battles incurable cancer. *CBS*. Retrieved from http:// http://www.cbs46.com/story/19709925/hurricane-katrina-survivor-prepares-to

Tucker, A. (2003). Noesis: Comprehension and understanding- the autobiography of Alfonzo Tucker. California: R.A.W. Advantage.

Made in the USA
Columbia, SC
20 March 2021